The Law of Attraction

Game Book 2

Feel Great Being You:

A Daily Inspiration Workbook

PK Davies

JOYFUL LIFE MASTERY

JOYFUL LIFE MASTERY BOOKS

Copyright © 2021 by PK Davies

www.JoyfulLifeMastery.com

All rights reserved. No part of this publication may be reproduced, distributed, or transmitted in any form or by any means, including photocopying, recording, or other electronic or mechanical methods. Included are a few recommended affiliate links. At no additional cost to you, Joyful Life Mastery will earn a small commission if you decide to make a purchase after clicking through the link. These will help defray the cost of maintaining the Joyful Life Mastery website and your support is genuinely appreciated.

For information about special discounts for bulk purchases, please contact Joyful Life Mastery at JoyfulLifeMastery@gmail.com.

ISBN: 978-1-7776613-4-2

Book Website and Newsletter:

Joyfullifemastery.com

Socia Media:

Facebook.com/joyfullifemastery

PRAISE FOR GAME BOOK 1:

MARISSA STAPLEY, BEST-SELLING AUTHOR, *Things to Do When It's Raining*

"Wonderfully enlightening. I just loved this book. (PK Davies') writing style is inspiring, kind and gently persuasive. It feels like having a conversation with a good friend and contained many lessons about manifesting and living my best life that I'm going to carry with me. Highly recommend!"

JOSHUA CINTRON, AUTHOR & PUBLISHER, *Upon a Moonlight Kiss*

"The material in this book is life changing. This book is a system, a way of life."

PHILIPPA SETTELS, OWNER & FOUNDER of B green

"The Law of Attraction Game Book 28 days of Love' is a delight to read! As adults surrounded by responsibilities, we tend to forget to play sometimes! This gem of a book is the perfect way to start having a little more fun in life and brings the LOA front and center with joy, love and light."

READER'S FAVOURITE (5 STARS)

"...As I read through this little gem of a book, I was struck by the imagination and love of life that went into each day's offering. The first day's subject alone had me thinking about things in an entirely new and positive light... Law of Attraction Game Book: 28 Days of Love is most highly recommended."

AMAZON UK (5 STARS)

"I love this book. I am really enjoying the daily tasks, I look forward every day to see what is ahead for the day. I feel this book is making me appreciate my body and character. I have read lots of books on the law of attraction but this one really holds my interest, it is refreshingly different, this is a book I will read over and over again until I feel I understand the tasks fully."

ANDREW MARC ROWE, AUTHOR

"I'd recommend this book to anyone with an open mind and who is looking to create a kinder, gentler reality for themselves. Because we are all *it*, people! The ones we've been waiting for. Billions of creators running around this blue and green ball of ours. Better we create beauty than the opposite. And Khajuria's book will help you on the path to do just this."

"Give yourself a gift of five minutes of contemplation in awe of everything you see around you. Go outside and turn your attention to the many miracles around you. This five-minute-a-day regimen of appreciation and gratitude will help you to focus your life in awe."

WAYNE DYER

Ignite
THE PATH TO A MAGICAL LIFE

Manifesting should be fun!

We know that life, change and transformation can carry their own types of growing pains.

All the more reason to make the process of transformation enjoyable.

Jump into an adventure like no other...

IGNITE: The Path to a Magical Life

Go on fun manifesting Quests, each of which will transform your life.
PLUS collect surprise manifesting gifts, trophies and badges after each Quest.

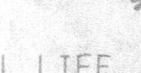

Ignite
THE PATH TO A MAGICAL LIFE

Each Joyful Life Mastery offering will give you the link to start Quest 1 for FREE. There is no obligation to continue.

However, if you decide you're ready for this adventure...

In only a few short months, your family, friends and colleagues will be amazed at the changes in your life.

But more importantly, you'll be living with a sense of poise, joyful adventure and clarity – and creating your magical life, step-by-step.

Whether you choose to sample the Joyful Life offerings a la carte or dive straight into this exciting adventure, I wish you so much inspiration, fun and happiness on your journey!

With much love,

PK Davies

Quest 1
THE COSMIC PLAYBOOK

Journey to Joy...

Daily inspiration to power your journey. Mini meditations, affirmations and intentions that spark loving mindfulness and self-awareness each day.

Visit and sign up at:
www.JoyfulLifeMastery.com

Start the Quest 1 in your adventure for FREE.

Quest 3
THE LAW OF ATTRACTION GAME BOOK 2

Journey to Joy...

Dive deep into a world of appreciation and inspiration. Learn an emotional soothing technique to supercharge your alignment.

At the end of The Law of Attraction Game Book 2, you will find your secret link and magic password to collect your surprise gift and your Quest 3 trophy.

Ignite
THE PATH TO A
MAGICAL LIFE

Table of Contents

Introduction: Everything Starts with You!...............1

The Power of The Mindful Pause............................5

Day 5 - Love Your Accomplishments..................... 28

Day 6 - Your Kindness 29

Day 7 – Enhancing Qualities 30

Day 8 - A New Appreciation 33

Day 9 - Your Laugh 34

Day 10 - Meet Your Higher Self............................. 36

Day 11 - Love Your Face 40

Day 12 - Love Your Hair & Head 43

Day 13 - Love Your Body.. 45

Day 14 - The Joy of Quirkiness 47

Day 15 - Love Your Skin 48

Day 16 - Your Voice 51

Day 17 - Family... 53

Day 18 - Friends 54

Day 19 - Animals 55

Day 20 - Home 56

Day 21 - Work..57

Day 22 - Surroundings.. 58

Day 23 - City... 59

Day 24 - Your Stuff.. 62

Day 25 - The Great Outdoors 63

Day 26 - The Past 65

Day 27 - The Future 66

Day 28 - The Present... 68

Thank You! 85

About PK Davies 87

Introduction: Everything Starts with You!

"To accept yourself fully in the present moment, knowing that you are a marvelous work-in-progress yet an infinite Divine spark of Life itself, is one of the greatest forms of self-love."

PK DAVIES

elcome, beautiful Soul!

This is Book 2 that follows and expands on *The Law of Attraction Game Book: 28 Days of Love*. If you haven't read that yet, I highly recommend starting with Book 1.

It sets the stage for self-love and appreciation with PROOF, and guides you into the Daily Power Ritual that aligns you with this proof and also boosts self-confidence.

You can get a copy of Book 1 by visiting:
https://amzn.to/3CsY4rF

In Game Book 2, you're going to go deeper into the *same* categories from Book 1.
MUCH deeper.
You'll experience some of the most inspiring aspects of your life and you will feel fantastic about yourself!

Let's recap a few important things to set the stage...

Sorrow, sadness and painful experiences are part of Life. We know this.
But Life also includes joyful experiences, heartfelt connections, beauty, love and fun!

There are enough reminders of tragedy coming in from the outside. Without bypassing life, we can accept that they happen.

But how we respond to unavoidably unfortunate situations and experiences can also make us stronger so we can live mindfully, compassionately and lovingly.

We can stand up for those who need help, we can share our voices.
And we can still live a richly creative life.

Yes, we will screw up sometimes in our lives (hey, we all do).
Yes, we will make mistakes along the way (it's perfectly fine).

But from these, we will build courage and resilience.
And as we do that, we FEEL our inner strength building.

We can do both – respond to the negative aspects in our world and life by using our voice to stand up for our Earth, for others and human rights.

And we can also illuminate the beauty that is working in our lives.
Both are true. Both exist.

We're going to shine light into the beautiful aspects of your life by implementing the Master tools of Loving Kindness all through this book!

Alright, my friend, are you ready?
Woot woot, let's gooooo!

THE MINDFUL PAUSE: THE JOYFUL LIFE 7-STEP FORMULA

Ooh, the pause…
Let's talk about where to best use it and how.

When something happens in our life that we don't love, we normally either react or respond. Sometimes, we ignore it.

The *mindful pause* is what helps to add space and time between the experience and what you choose to do next.

I'm sure you've heard that saying that when something unpleasant happens, count to 10. Or perhaps you've read about Byron Katie's 4 questions that you ask yourself – also a powerful tool.

It's kind of like that. By hitting pause, it gives us a chance to reflect on what we're going to say or do next.

Adding a pause increases the chance that we'll *respond* and lessens the chance that we'll *react*. It allows us to temper the response/reaction with more thought into what happens next.

Whatever we "do or say next" is always happening in the present moment. And that sets the stage for what happens after that.

With a mindful pause, we can slip into a manifested version of what we want to experience and bridge the two. We can also do it in a way where we express ourselves more meaningfully.

To be clear, emotions are all good. Emotions are *life*. But if we react to unpleasant situations or interactions with heightened and strong emotions (anger, frustration) on a *continuous* basis, it affects our general day-to-day energy. This in turn affects what we manifest into our lives.

Again – to be *very* clear, anger and frustration are completely acceptable.

They can be powerful markers that direct us to what we do want to experience, without bypassing. We can use these to work towards justice and a better world for all of us.

We just want to assess how and when we're experiencing them, so we can take practical action as needed towards the best possible outcome.

We can use the mindful pause to direct all our emotions into words or actions that further our cause, with more clarity.

Here's the Joyful Life formula for using a Mindful Pause...

1. When something unwanted happens, take a deep breath as you count to 4. Hold your breath to the count of 4, then release it slowly.
2. Ask yourself: *Can I change what just happened?*

3. If not, accept it as an event that has happened in the past – you are not accepting the behaviour or situation itself per se.
4. If you *can* change it (perhaps it's unfolding right in front of you), ask yourself: *How can I change this for the highest good of all concerned, either for the present or for the future?*
5. Then respond with your thought / action for positive change. Yes, this may involve emotions.
6. Afterwards, take some sort of physical positive action to move the emotions through safely (sports, dance, kick a pillow, go for a fast walk or run, etc.).
7. And then get back to living – refocusing your attention on today's intentions and actions.

Let's break this down, so you can see what is happening with each step...

Mindful Pause

When something unpleasant happens, take a deep breath as you count to 4.

You're filling your lungs with refreshing oxygen.

According to *UW Medicine* "Deep breathing (sometimes called diaphragmatic breathing) is a practice that enables more air to flow into your body and can help calm your nerves, reducing stress and anxiety. It can also help you improve your attention span and lower pain levels."

You're also drawing in fresh energy.

Hold your breath to the count of 4, then release it slowly.

According to *Kristoffer Rhoads, Ph.D.*, a clinical neuropsychologist who treats patients at the Memory & Brain Wellness Center at Harborview Medical Center, "Breathing more deeply also allows for more carbon dioxide to enter your blood, which quiets down parts of the brain, like the amygdala, that handle your anxiety response. More carbon dioxide also helps synchronize your heartbeat and breathing."

These first 2 steps are part of ancient yogic breathing practices – well known and proven over thousands of years to help reset ourselves and enter into presence.

Ask yourself: *Can I change what just happened?*

In this very moment, you are taking a step back and looking at the situation from a distance.
You're also showing respect to your inner self by "consulting" with yourself.

If you can't change it, accept it as an event that has happened in the past – you're not accepting the behavior or situation itself per se.

You're giving yourself a breather here.
And you're taking down the emotional fire just a touch, so you can again look at it a bit more clearly.

If you *can* change it (as perhaps it's unfolding right in front of you), ask yourself: *How can I change this for the highest good of all concerned, either for the present or for the future?*

You're continuing to assess first. You're then viewing this from a greater perspective - the higher perspective - and with your natural compassion. You are incorporating this event into a catalyst for good, without bypassing Life.

Then respond with your thought / action for positive change.

You're now igniting your creative spark and harnessing the power of your own potential by blending action with Universal compassion.

This might involve a very clear conversation, or taking action from creating some sort of resolution all the way to working towards human rights and equality.

Afterwards, take some sort of physical positive action to move the emotions through safely (sports, dance, kick a pillow, etc.)

All emotions find their way into our body, our muscles and organs. Our mind, body, spirit and emotions are all connected.

Taking some sort of safe physical action helps push that energy back out through your body in a healthy way, so you can rest afterwards and recoup your vitality.

And then get back to living – refocusing your attention on today's intentions and actions.

You have now taken an unwanted situation, and applied your creativity to change something about it for the highest good.

This has changed the natural timeline of the event (the tail end) and you can now reinvest your energy back into the Now.

There are many tools to help restabilize emotional wellness...

EFT

You may have heard of EFT (the Emotional Freedom Technique) that blends mindful affirmations with acupressure-type tapping. This technique blends statements with affirmations and the tapping.

VAM

VAM or Vibrational Alignment Mastery is what I call the intuitive and mystical feminine divine version of EFT. There's an introduction to this practice at the end of the book as a bonus, along with examples.

Music

Music can be one the most powerful ways to rebalance or tweak emotions.
Who hasn't been moved to joy or tears through the magic of melody and music?

It's normal to create a favorite playlist. However, I suggest to also create a couple of playlists based on emotional context. (i.e. joyful music, peaceful music, rock, metal, etc). And then use these playlists consciously when you need them!

Meditation

Meditation is one of the most universally popular ways to balance and rejuvenate emotions and vibrations. It's also one of the most ancient.
Meditation does not have to be only breathing or chanting.

It can be mindful practice. It can be an audible focusing practice, such as by using affirmations.

Set aside an hour for yourself one day where you simply research and test types of meditations.
You can test out various apps, or have fun checking out Youtube videos.

Creative Pursuits

Occupying yourself with creative projects and tasks brings your attention into the Now moment and helps redirect your attention to your creative powers – from something as simple as preparing a meal to the more complex activities of creating art or anything you enjoy.

Play

One of the most exciting and fun ways to reboot joy is through play – this is also the one activity we tend to bypass the most as adults. Sports can be a form of joyful play too, however the competitive aspect changes that element somewhat.
Dancing and other simple playful activities without any end goal are liberating and joyful.

And now, my friend…let's begin with the Game Book.

How to Play

As I mentioned earlier, the book you're reading is a deep dive into each topic from Book 1.

You're going to go further, and the revelations about yourself will be exciting!

There will be fun little exercises and some journaling prompts. You're going to be unraveling and discovering. And you'll also jump into creating and manifesting!
All you need is about 5-10 minutes a day...

Set up a daily Calendar reminder at a time that you'll have a little privacy.

Keep a notebook and pen handy too.

Day 1 - Love Your Mind

Visualization exercise:

You've had a long day at work and it pretty much sucked. You decide to go for a walk in the park to get a bit of fresh air and enjoy some time to yourself.

The sun is still shining, and you begin to feel better. You breathe in the refreshing air deeply and relax into the peace and quiet.

On your way, you discover a path leading off into another direction - one that you hadn't noticed before. The path gently meanders around another corner and you find yourself in a small forest.

The trees are taller here, closer together and so very lush. As you walk through this forest with wonder, you notice a small hut.

There's a little plaque on the front of the hut...it belongs to the park and seems to be public. But there's no one inside. The door is open, so you walk in and look around.

The hut smells fragrant and feels warm, as though a cozy fire has just been put out. In a corner of the room, there's a desk with a pad of paper and a pen. A computer sits there as well, still running.

What do you do next?

1. You quickly walk outside and hurry back up the path. You don't know whose hut it is, and you sure don't want to be caught trespassing.
2. You walk over to the pad of paper and begin to doodle. After doodling, you make a checklist of

things you have to remember. You add a grocery list and put the paper in your pocket.
3. You sit down at the computer, log into a browser and google this area. You want to know what this hut and area is all about.

The Reveal:

The forest represents the unconscious mind, a rich inner world of growth and mystery.

If you chose 1, this reveals that you feel most comfortable right now with the safety of an orderly and predictable routine. You may fear meeting new people or discovering the next step to take in your life.

This might be because of habit, stuckness, indecision, or because you have hidden doubts when it comes to trying new things. (And let's not forget the pandemic!)

- What would you like to try one day, something that's not part of your usual routine?
- What's holding you back?

- Imagine yourself trying this new activity…and then plan it and do it! If you like, ask a friend to join you!
- If it's funds that are holding you back, open an account just for Adventures and put aside a couple of bucks each pay.

If you chose 2, this reveals that you are very much a doer but may be caught up in the whirlwind of daily activity. You have a playful side, but you feel play has to wait until the "real work" is done.

You have artistic projects on the backburner that you often think about. But there never seems to be enough time for them.

There are dreams you want to attain, milestones you're yearning to reach, and you don't feel "complete" yet.

- Pick one artistic or creative project that you've been thinking about.
- What could you do, to start today?
- Could you clear a space on your desk or in your home for this project?

- Could you find time in your schedule for just 15 minutes a day?
- How would you feel if you could "be" in the flow of your new project, even for just 15 minutes a day?

If you chose 3, you're on the verge of a new and exciting time. You like to explore and take action. You want to get your hands into your life as much as possible. You have a thirst for knowledge, and there is a bit of an adventurer in you.

Sometimes you have a tendency to spread yourself a little thin by planning many things at the same time. You get stronger and clearer when you focus on one project at a time.

- Which one desire, goal, project or plan are you the most excited about right now?
- How would you plan the first 3 steps towards it?
- What could you start today?

Day 2 – Compliments For Others

This is an incredible way to ramp up some major high vibes...

Set up a daily Calendar reminder for the next 10 days. Add each of these into the Calendar, one per day:

1. Find something about yourself to compliment. Start small or GO BIG!
2. Tell your child (or a friend) about something lovely you noticed in them.
3. Tell your spouse (or friend) about something wonderful you noticed about them.
4. Thank your colleague for something and let them know 1 thing you appreciate about them.

5. Give a stranger a compliment at the grocery store.
6. Do you take the bus or train to work? Give someone you normally see there a compliment and watch their eyes shine!
7. Compliment your pet! They'll understand your vibration as you say it!
8. Call your mother or father (or a loved parental figure) and give them a sincere compliment at the end of your chat.
9. Text your brother, sister or best friend and give them a compliment.
10. Post a compliment on a friend's Facebook page, for all to see.

DAY 3 - SELF-CARE

Create a journaling list under each heading: *Body, Mind, and Spirit.*

For example, under *Body*, note down all the things you love to do to refresh your body.

- Do you enjoy massages?
- How about a spa visit?
- Do you love mani-pedis?
- Maybe you enjoy taking a relaxing walk in nature?
- Perhaps you have fun when you visit the gym, or take a dance class?
- Do you love a refreshing nap?
- Do you love juicing or smoothies?

- Or perhaps a night out with friends really relaxes you?

For now, don't worry about the pandemic restrictions and what you're able to do at this time.

Simply write down everything you can, then do the same for *Mind* and *Spirit*. Some items may overlap and that's okay.

I love reading uplifting and motivational books or articles when I can. In the evenings, I wind down with my family, watch a fun show, read a book or practice singing.

When the weather is good, I go for a walk on the waterfront to re-energize. Write down what *you* love, and don't judge any of it!

Once your list is complete, set up a daily Calendar reminder prompt for the mornings.

Glance at your list every day when you get that prompt and ask yourself: *Which of these would I like to do today?*

Day 4 - Cool things About You

Complete the following sentence in your journal:

If I could give myself a medal for something, it would be because I (fill this in).

Come up with at least 10 items.

Once you're done, read through your list.
Rest in the warm feeling of all that you have already achieved.

Feel excitement about what lies ahead.

You are awesome!

Day 5 - Love Your Accomplishments

Today, you have 3 journal prompts...

- Which of your favorite accomplishments did you manifest from beginning to end *consciously*? Which ones did you see in your mind's eye *before* or *as* you started? Make a list.

- Which ones were particularly satisfying to achieve? Why?

- How did it make you feel about yourself? Jot down the emotions or write with description.

Day 6 - Your Kindness

This is a 3-day exercise.

Write down what you did for each of the items below, and jot down how it made you feel.

1) Do something kind for a family member.
2) Offer a kind word to someone at work.
3) Say something kind to a stranger.

Day 7 – Enhancing Qualities

Here is a fun exercise that shows that we enhance what we focus on. Read it through first, and then try it.

Look straight ahead and let your attention relax. Let your vision relax as well.

Now say to yourself *blue* a couple of times while still gazing gently forward. Without turning around to consciously look for blue objects, the most amazing thing will happen without moving your eyes.

Blue items in your room or vicinity will slowly begin to pop into your peripheral vision.

Now say to yourself *red*. Red and pink items will now reveal themselves in your peripheral vision and other colors will fade back slightly.

You can try this with objects, such as cars when you're outside, or even textures and senses. I've said words like *sensation* and instantly become aware of the wind against my skin and the feeling of the pavement under my shoes.

I once repeated the word *wealth* when I was on a walk. Instantly a plethora of trees around me stood out along with the marina. Everything else faded into the background.

As it happens, trees are part of nature's abundance. And a marina is considered a sign of prosperity in the ancient Chinese energy flow system of Feng Shui!

We are surrounded by countless stimuli and objects. Yet our conscious awareness can only take in so much at any one time. If you say a word, and that item really isn't in your current vicinity, keep an eye out for how soon you *do* find it afterwards!

Your attention and focus enhance what is already there within the bigger picture and brings it forward to you more clearly.

Recognizing and contemplating the qualities of those you admire will enhance those already-existing qualities in yourself.

Day 8 - A New Appreciation

Today involves a journal prompt...

Think back through the day and jot down at least 3 answers to the following...

Today, I really appreciate (fill in the blank) about myself!

No judging – just go for it!

Day 9 - Your Laugh

Let's talk about your laugh...

- What makes you giggle? What makes you laugh?
- Which is the last book you read that made you laugh? (Mine was *the 100-Year-Old Man Who Climbed Out the Window and Disappeared* by Jonas Jonasson)
- What was the most recent movie or TV show that made you laugh? (mine was the TV series *Rutherford Falls*)
- Which of your friends or relatives laugh the most, and make you laugh as well?
- There is something fun and quirky about yourself that makes you laugh. What is it?

- What do you love about your laugh?

To attract more fun and funny experiences, do more of those things that make you laugh! Spend more time being around those who laugh regularly or who make you laugh.

Or perhaps *you* are the funny one who creates laughter around you...if so, bring more of that into your life and offer it to those around you.

Watch that electric energy build and transform into sheer vitality.
Feel it expand into warm, loving, human connection!

Day 10 - Meet Your Higher Self

In this gentle heart-light exercise, you're going to meet with your Higher Self.

Who is your Higher Self?
It's the bigger, deeper, inner part of you that is aligned with the vastness of cosmic consciousness.

It's your inner Divinity that transcends time or religion. Your Higher Self is the aspect of you that remains unaffected by the drama of life. And it watches over you with boundless love.

Your Higher Self *loves* you as you are and *accepts* you and your past unconditionally. Your Higher Self is there to accompany you through all your life experiences.

(Note: Feel free to replace the words Higher Self with God, Goddess, Spirit or whatever you personally relate to).

Take a deep breath and hold it for a second, then blow it out. Repeat this twice.
Now bring your attention to your heart center. Imagine a luminous white light filling your heart area.

Let it continue to shine and rest there for a few moments. Keep your focus on your heart area and the soft light as it continues to expand.

You may begin to feel a slight surge of energy from your navel upwards.

Send out an intention to engage with your Higher Self. To do this, simply ask to connect. Allow the light to flow upwards from your heart and out through the top of your head. You can say a few words out loud if you like, asking your Higher Self to connect with you now.

You may receive images in your mind of your Higher Self with a certain physical form. Or you may feel an increasing sense of warmth or comfort.

Ask your Higher Self now to bring your attention to your lovable qualities.

Cast your mind back and reach for loving things you have thought, said or done over the years. Allow your mind to gently sift through memories as they arise. If something unrelated or unpleasant comes up, envision it as a little puff of mist and gently blow it away.

Continue reaching for loving experiences. Think about love that you have given freely to someone. Love that you have shared with others. Loving thoughts that you have felt. Loving things that you have done.

Gifts that you've given with innocence and generosity.

You may feel more joyful surges of energy from your solar plexus. If your mind wanders off track, simply allow it for a moment and then gently bring your attention back.

Contemplate and rest in this experience for as long as you can and for as long as it feels good. Once you feel fully refreshed, thank your Higher Self and send it love.

Send out waves of kindness and understanding to your past self.

Hold a deepening space of compassionate acceptance for your present self.

Send out warm and loving encouragement to the future YOU and relax.

Day 11 - Love Your Face

We all have sensitivities about our looks. Whatever you feel is okay.

Just remember that the standards of "looks" vary wildly from culture to culture. Our looks can change from day to day, year to year and we can come to love it at any time in our life.

Today, we're going to give some massive love to "this face" no matter the conditions or circumstances.

Look at yourself in the mirror.

At first, your eyes will be darting over all your features, sometimes assessing, sometimes judging.

Let it flow at will.

Let the assessments flow through you.
Let the judgements flow through you.
Let them flow...and let them go.

After these work their way through, continue gazing at yourself.
Just rest in the space, this time, this Now moment.

And look deeply into your own eyes. Softy, gently.
And send yourself waves of compassion, love and caring.

Remain like this for as long as you can.

I recommend doing the mirror technique for several days in a row, preferably 21 to 30 days. Louise Hay, the founder of Hay House books, was a pioneer in holistic healing education.

She credits mirror work as being one of the most powerful techniques to learn to love oneself, and it was one that she practiced regularly.

There are many ways to use this technique. Simply look at yourself in the mirror each day and express appreciation to yourself.

If your day was good, congratulate yourself while looking into your eyes in the mirror.
If it wasn't that good of a day, soothe yourself and tell yourself gently that tomorrow will be better.

The classic technique involves looking at yourself in the mirror in the morning and evening, and saying ***I love you*** to your reflection. That's it.

This simple act creates a momentum of connection with yourself and it deepens over time. The more you practice this looking at your reflection, the more you connect with the "you" behind your reflection.

Set up a Calendar reminder and try the mirror technique daily for as long as it feels good.

Day 12 - Love Your Hair & Head

This is an exercise your hair and scalp will love!

Place your hands on both sides of your head with the fingers pointing towards the back of your head. Place the heels of your palms at the sides of your forehead, over your ears.

Gently apply a little pressure to your scalp and move your palms in a circular manner so that they're gently massaging your head. Move your hands higher up and continue. Then lightly massage the top of your head.

Place your focus and awareness on each area that you're massaging. Now place your hands under your ears and massage the bottom areas of your head.

Once you are completely done, use the tips of your fingers to lightly tap all over your head in a quick, pressing manner.
Once you are done, your scalp should feel fresh and energized, yet relaxed.

You can kick this exercise up a notch by applying a little massage oil to your scalp. Pick an oil that is safe for the head area and for your hair.

Apply the oil gently into the scalp and through the hair. Do the massage and leave the oil on your head for an hour.
Then wash, shampoo and condition as usual.

Day 13 - Love Your Body

Mentally scan your body from head to foot and send thoughts of love and appreciation to each part of you.

Is there a part of your body that you're unhappy with?

Then send that area even MORE love and attention.

Say to your body:

I accept you!
I appreciate you so much!
Thank you for everything you did for me yesterday!
Thanks for serving me all night as I sleep.
I love you, my body.

My beautiful body, each day you get stronger, healthier and more vibrant!

Thank you for everything that you do!

Thank you for being here with me through this lifetime!

Day 14 - The Joy of Quirkiness

Run your mind through a list of close family and friends.

Think about which of their quirks make them so lovable.

- What are some fun quirks of one of your friends?
- Think about a family member – what are their funny and cute quirks?
- How about those of your pet, or a friend's pet?

Day 15 - Love Your Skin

Here's an exercise that will change the way you see your skin.

Set aside 5-10 minutes today at home when you have privacy.

Undress to the extent that you are comfortable. I suggest stripping entirely.

Once you're ready, gaze down at your skin. Really notice it. You can look at your skin in the mirror as well, if you like.

Again, as in any part of these exercises, if judgements arise, accept them in the moment and gently release them.

As you gaze at your skin, gently run your fingertips down your body. Start from your forehead and run your fingertips around your eyes and down over your nose.

Trail your fingertips over your lips, over your throat and continue like this all the way down your body from your head to your toes.

It may feel very strange the first time or so.
This exercise, however, will unlock the most wonderful appreciation of your skin.

You can use both hands if you like, to gently trail your fingertips over as much of your skin as you please.

It might tickle, and you may find yourself smiling uncontrollably. Our skin was meant to be touched. It loves to be caressed (with your permission)!

As you run your fingertips down your body, send your skin some warm love.

You can say the following blessing out loud, or simply read it to yourself:

Thank you.
I love you!
I love everything you do for me
I love how you protect me
I love how you feel
I love how good it feels when something soft touches you!
I adore the feeling of seaside breezes on you!
I love the warmth of the sun on you.
I love how you serve me day and night, and when I sleep
I love how healthy and firm and vibrant you are!

Day 16 - Your Voice

You're going to send love to your throat area with this little exercise...

Visualize a warm golden light, infused with healing vibrations, expanding and growing in your heart area. This light is Love. Simply rest with this for a few moments and then amplify the sensation.

Now gently move this light upwards into your throat area and let it circulate in a clockwise direction. Continue this for as long as you can.

Imagine the light expanding outwards and filling every nook and cranny in your throat, healing and energizing. Allow the light to move upwards through the back of your throat, clearing your sinus path.

Feel the warmth infusing the path from your heart to your throat.

From this moment onwards, your true intentions and emotions will flow with increasing clarity, confidence and freedom through your voice.

Know that your voice is a gift to yourself and the world around you. See yourself filling your voice with love and light each morning.

If you are a speaker, voice actor or singer – bless and thank your voice.

Send it love and gratitude for being your faithful and loving friend and partner.

Day 17 – Family

Think back, and bring to mind someone whom you bonded and connected with as family in all the ways that are meaningful to you. Someone who had the most positive impact on your life.

If this person is still in your life, consider sending them a handwritten note in a card.

Or send them an email, a text or give them a call to let them know how much they mean to you.

If they have passed on, write a note anyway and keep it in a journal as a sweet and potent reminder of the beauty and inspiration you received from them.

Their energy will live on with you!

Day 18 - Friends

Think about someone whose friendship you cherish. Someone who inspires you, and has always been there to support you.

Contact this friend today by phone, text or email and let them know how much you appreciate them.

For extra love-points, consider posting your appreciation somewhere on their social media.

Day 19 - Animals

If you have pets, cuddle them in your arms and send warm, loving energy from your heart center.

Gaze at your pet with your full loving attention. See their place within your arms, your room, your home, your family - as a companion in your lifetime in this body.

Feel them breathing in your arms, enjoy their texture and their comforting weight in your hands.

Rest in this beautiful moment of love.

Day 20 - Home

Today, walk into each of your rooms and just spend a moment sensing the space that surrounds you.

It's perfectly normal if you find yourself suddenly coming up with a to-do list.
If that happens, smile and grab a notebook!

Make your list, and just let the words flow.
Then place your notebook and pen down – and sense the space again.

Send out warm, soothing, loving energy around you. Visualize this energy reaching into all the corners of your home and building more love and warmth.

Day 21 - Work

Today, give yourself a challenge and look for something "extra" to do.

Something that would be above and beyond your normal work activity.
Something to contribute to your work tasks, your office, or to a colleague.

Offer some extra help or send a supportive email to thank one of your work mates.

Pick one thing today that brings in the energy of *loving kindness*.

Day 22 - Surroundings

Today brings you journal prompts about your surroundings...

- What are you situated close to, that you love?
- A park, maybe, where you can relax?
- Are you near other enjoyable amenities?
- Or perhaps you enjoy easy access to work?
- What else do you really appreciate in your vicinity?
- If you're at work right now, what is it that you love about the location or the surroundings?

Day 23 - City

Search for your city on Wikipedia. Or Google "the best of (your city name)." For fun, read through everything you find.

Then send out love and appreciation to all who have made your city a very special place...

- Whoever designed and built your streets.
- Those who planted trees and who take care of the city landscaping.
- The people who clean the streets.
- The owners and clerks who operate the stores that you love to visit.

- The restaurants and the people who cook the meals you love, those who serve you, and the ones who clean.

- The engineers who designed your transit system. The bus and subway operators.

- Your city support system that fixes everything, or those who remove the garbage.

- Those who designed, built and operate your community services. The pools, the classes, the gyms, the parks.

- The hospitals and medical offices in your city.

- The hotels, the sports and concert stadiums and places of leisure.

- The cozy spaces that you love.

- The artists that bring imagination, design, color and beauty to your senses.

- The musicians that bring your city to life.

- And anyone else that comes to mind – you'll think of more each time you play!

To anything and everything in your city - just say:
Thank you, I love you!

(If you're living in a less than ideal area, google a place you would love to visit and do this exercise imagining that you are there.)

Day 24 - Your Stuff

Today is the day to appreciate your things. Yes, to love your stuff!

Physically touch your belongings. Touch the things in your office, the items in your rooms at home.

Gently touch the clothes in your closets, your coats, your shoes, clothing in drawers, your curtains.

Trail your hand lightly over all your things as you walk from room to room.

As you do so, just say:

Thank you, I love you for being with me!
Thank you for being part of my home and my life!
Thank you, I love you!

Day 25 - The Great Outdoors

Today, we look at the beautiful world outside.

- Which cities, places and countries are you drawn to?
- What is it about each of them that fascinate you?
- Which would you love to visit in person?
- Which place would you love to visit first?

Google everything you can about the place you'd love to visit first on your list and open a folder on your desktop. For extra fun, see if you can find a Facebook group dedicated for lovers of that city or location, and join it.

Search for anything about this location that inspires you, including flight or travel costs to get there, best hotel reviews, restaurants, sightseeing and other things to enjoy. Save these links.

Open a Word document and add your own notes. They'll come in handy one day! You can also use a tracking system.

Save pictures to your desktop, or place them into a digital vision board (a simple Word document or your desktop will work fine).

Most importantly, **revel in the feelings.** Feel that you're enjoying this trip in the here and now as you're going through all the research online.

Day 26 - The Past

Today, you have some fun journal prompts...

- What are some of your best memories?
- What's one of the best decisions you've ever made?
- What are some of the best concerts or shows you can remember attending?
- What are some of the most fun times you've had till now?
- What are some of the best vacations you've been on?
- What did you do last month that was exciting?
- How about last week?
- What did you do or experience yesterday that was wonderful?

Day 27 - The Future

Today you have more juicy journal prompts...

1. Make a list by *week*, *month* and *year* of your upcoming events and save them in an email draft or in a document.
2. Create a separate list called *To Book*.
3. Add upcoming ideas, concerts and trips to the *To Book* document.
4. Add dates to your Calendar to remind yourself to take action on the *To Book* items, or to take the next inspired action step towards them.
5. Add them into your budget.
6. Add to your lists whenever new events get booked.

By the way, don't add any appointment that you're not excited about onto these lists. Keep them in your scheduler instead. These lists are only for enjoyable events and dates.

Each time you look at your lists, you'll feel anticipation and excitement!

Day 28 - The Present

And here we are, my friend...

THIS....is your moment of power.

Notice the colors around you.

Listen to the sounds.

Feel the space around you.

Breathe in deeply.

Touch anything next to you and really feel the sensation under your fingertips.

Today, you are vibrant and alive!

"We cannot always control our thoughts, but we can control our words, and repetition impresses the subconscious, and we are then master of the situation."

Florence Scovel Shinn

"One comes to believe whatever one repeats to oneself sufficiently often, whether the statement be true or false. It comes to be dominating thought in one's mind."

Robert Collier

"It's the repetition of affirmations that leads to belief.
And once that belief becomes a deep conviction, things begin to happen."

Claude M. Bristol

BONUS SECTION:

INTRODUCTION TO VIBRATIONAL

ALIGNMENT MASTERY

Vibrational Alignment Mastery (VAM)

Vibrational Alignment Mastery (VAM) is a powerful, spiritual healing technique that combines:

- the verbal techniques of EFT (Emotional Freedom Technique)
- Law of Attraction spiritual principles
- ancient Chakra energy alignment
- elements of reiki
- heart-centred and intuitive grounding techniques

This technique helps reduce limiting beliefs and boost beneficial beliefs.

It's also a highly effective self-soothing technique.

This version – which I call the feminine divine version of EFT – blends the EFT affirmation-narrative aspect with more of an embrace-and-gentle-touch aspect.

How To Use VAM

In this section, you'll learn how to use VAM as a quick way to self-soothe and for anything that troubles you.

We'll also use VAM in the context of self-love.

With VAM, you'll gently place your hands on certain areas of your body and express any troublesome issues, and then invite in self-acceptance and what you desire.

There are 4 asanas (poses) with VAM.

I use the yogic term *asana*, as there is a flow and presence to an asana that cannot be fully expressed when using a term such as "pose." Pose implies a stationary position, which these do have. But the asanas include intentional flow and energy.

Though this may sound a little strange at the moment, if you're familiar with yoga, you'll understand what I mean. And using VAM yourself will express this in action.

With the Vibrational Mastery Flow, we are moving from the head to the belly. From thought to emotion.

Let's look at the asanas first, then we'll energize them with the flow sequence...

Asana 1 – The Blessing

Place your right hand on top of your head and palm your left hand over your forehead.

This connects your crown and third eye chakras. The hand on top of the head is the universal pose of ancestral blessings and goodwill.

With this asana, you're inviting in the blessings of your ancestors, and joining it with your blessing to yourself. The third eye opens your intuition with connection.

Asana 2 – The Cradle

Place your hands gently on both sides of your face. Feel the warmth or the coolness of your palms. This is the loving caress of lover to lover.

It is also the way a parent may hold their beloved child's face.

It invites in tenderness and loving kindness.

Asana 3 – The Heart-Connect

Place your right hand gently on your throat and your left hand on your heart.

This asana powerfully boosts energy between your heart and your "voice."

It connects your throat and heart chakras.

Asana 4 – The Core-Caress

Place both hands on your belly, as though you are embracing it.

This asana links and stimulates the energy between your sacral and solar plexus chakras.

It is a pose of self-soothing and utter self-acceptance.

The Emotion-Intentions

Just as in EFT, it's always best to verbalize what is truly bothering you, or the block that is preventing you from living fully, authentically or joyfully right now.

Step 1:

Verbalize anything that is bothering you, starting it with the phrase "Even though..." and end it with the phrase "I deeply and completely love and accept myself."

Here are some examples:

Even though I feel a bit depressed these days, I deeply and completely love and accept myself.

Even though I feel really bad about that argument, I deeply and completely love and accept myself.

Even though I am SO mad at (so-and-so), I deeply and completely love and accept myself.

Even though I think (so-and-so) is acting like a selfish bugger, I deeply and completely love and accept myself.

(Let it all out!)

Rewording whatever is bothering you with "even though" at the beginning allows you to step back a tiny bit to observe the situation.

Keep doing several rounds of the asanas while verbalizing any emotions at their strongest.

After a round or two, you'll notice your emotions beginning to diffuse. This is NOT bypassing – you're accepting your emotions fully (as you should). It is the *act* of self-acceptance that begins to diffuse the emotional intensity!

Step 2:

Allow this step to fall into place naturally – it will.
As the emotional tension begins to diffuse, change the wording accordingly.

Here are some examples:

I don't feel so depressed right now. And I deeply and completely love and accept myself.

Even though I feel a bit guilty about how I argued, it's good that I said what I needed to. And I deeply and completely love and accept myself.

Well (so-and-so) is their own person. Things will work out soon. And I deeply and completely love and accept myself.

I can't change (so-and-so). They're going to do what they're going to do. All I can do is share my side when necessary. Oh, and I deeply and completely love and accept myself!

(However you word it, is fine!)

The Flow

Now, we put it all together...

Start by breathing deeply three times.
Imagine or visualize Universal healing light energy entering your head at the crown.

Picture it as a golden ball of soft, shimmering light. Within this light is the Source energy of all that is beautiful and loving.

Allow it to travel down through each of your chakras - crown, third eye, throat, heart, solar plexus, sacral and out through your root chakra.

This light links each of your chakras. Think of lights turning on at night down a runway, one after the other, allowing aircraft to find its way.

Allow this light energy to flow through you for the duration of your technique.

After you have allowed this light to circulate freely through your body, move into the first asana *The Blessing*.

Allow the energy to move through your arms and hands and into your skin.

Verbalize the emotion-intentions either out loud or in your mind.

Move into the second asana *The Cradle*. Visualize the Universal light flowing through your hands and into your face as you hold your head with loving kindness.

Continue with the emotion-intentions.

Move into the third asana *The Heart-Connect*. Visualize the Universal light flowing through your arms and linking your heart and throat with soothing energy.

Continue with the emotion-intentions.

Move into the fourth asana *The Core-Caress*.
Visualize the Universal light flowing through your arms and deep into your belly into your organs and down through your thighs, legs and feet. Embrace your belly fully with loving kindness.

Continue with the emotion-intentions.

Now repeat a few rounds of the asanas and emotion-intentions until you feel much, much better (and you will!)

When you're ready, take a deep breath and stop.

VAM can also be used for affirmations and manifesting. Try it for a week with your favorite affirmations.

Use the VAM flow anywhere, at any time.

It's important to note that this works very well for a day-to-day self-soothing, rebalancing and re-energizing exercise.

But if you're experiencing any kind of trauma, abusive situation or suffer from ongoing depression – please reach out to a professional right away to receive clear and active support.

Thank You!

Yay, you made it to the end of the Game!!! Congratulations, my friend!

Thank you for reading, playing, journaling and being here in these moments together.

I wish for you a life filled with great joy, creativity and fulfillment.

May you shine your light bright and strong, beautiful soul!

With love,

PKDavies

Quest 3
THE LAW OF ATTRACTION GAME BOOK 2

YOUR SECRET LINK:

https://bit.ly/3K8MiWn

MAGIC PASSWORD:

VAMGuide

Ignite
THE PATH TO A
MAGICAL LIFE

About PK Davies

P.K. Davies creates award-winning Law of Attraction, manifesting and mindfulness products.
They are designed for those who want to forge their own path and create a fulfilling, empowered and expansive life filled with value and meaning.

Joyful Life Mastery tools combine metaphysical magic with down-to-earth goal achievement and a saucy passion for personal growth.

P.K. Davies is an author, voice artist and singer, with a degree in Psychology.
Born in England, she currently lives in Canada with her family.

Also by PK Davies:

THE COSMIC PLAYBOOK FOR WRITERS: Daily Affirmations And Mindfulness For Authors

SCENT OF AN ANGEL: POETRY – All about the angels in our lives.

Affirmations For Kids

THE FUN LETTER TRACING BOOKS VOL 1, 2, 3 - Joyful Letter Practice Workbooks For Preschool, Pre-K and Kindergarten Kids With Positive And Empowering Affirmations.

www.ingramcontent.com/pod-product-compliance
Lightning Source LLC
Chambersburg PA
CBHW070940080526
44589CB00013B/1588